Forget Me Not

– MARY JENNINGS –

An environmentally friendly book printed and bound in England by
www.printondemand-worldwide.com

Mixed Sources
Product group from well-managed
forests, and other controlled sources
www.fsc.org Cert no. TT-COC-002641
© 1996 Forest Stewardship Council

FSC

PEFC

PEFC/16-33-415

PEFC Certified
This product is
from sustainably
managed forests
and controlled
sources
www.pefc.org

This book is made entirely of chain-of-custody materials

i

www.fast-print.net/store.php

Forget Me Not
Copyright © Mary Jennings 2013

A catalogue record for this book is available from the British Library

ISBN 978-178035-719-5

First published 2013 by
FASTPRINT PUBLISHING
Peterborough, England.

Contents

Introduction

Twelve years ago I began to notice that my husband had a memory problem. Sadly he was recently admitted to long term residential care.

This is the story of the long journey through those 12 years, of the hopes and fears, of the humour and the sadness. It covers the difficulty of recognising when I needed help and the frustration of trying to get it when I became desperate. It is a tribute to the kindness and support of family and friends and the recognition of the dedication of many professionals who eventually became involved. It is also a criticism of a few who have been insensitive and indifferent, and at times, downright rude!

For many of those twelve years I have refused to use the word 'Alzheimer's' in connection with Norman's illness. There is no doubt that I was in denial. Eventually I looked into what literature was available at my local library to see if the symptoms and stages of Alzheimer 's disease corresponded with the behaviour I was witnessing from Norman. Since that time

Alzheimer's has become headline news as more and more people are diagnosed and more funding is directed into research around the disease. Information is much more readily available as there are newspaper articles and TV commentaries which link aspects of the disease. For anyone seeking easy to understand information about this devastating disease, there is no better place to start than with the Alzheimer's Society who have branches in most major towns and cities.

My own knowledge of why Norman developed Alzheimer's and the physiology of the disease is limited, but my experience of living with it is vast. Every carer will respond differently to the demands of a disease that eventually affects every aspect of their own lives as well as the person they care for. The carer's own lifestyle, temprement, health and mental stamina will determine how well, and indeed for how long, they can cope. This is just one woman's story.

Chapter 1:

About Us – Early Days

Norman and I met at a birthday party attended by a bright young crowd that made both of us feel very shy and awkward. We discussed the music of the time and discovered that we both liked dancing in the old romantic way. He invited me to the next village hop and we took it from there. During the interval Norman had no change to pay for the tea and buns and to this day still owes me two shillings and four pence. I'm not sure what this amount plus interest would be fifty seven years later!

Whilst we had lots in common there were fundamental differences in our personalities which probably kept the relationship from becoming stale. Perhaps the main difference was that Norman is a quiet, gentle man, generous to a fault, self-effacing and loved by everybody. Brought up in a God fearing village atmosphere by rather Victorian parents, his interests centered around church events and he was an active member of Kildwick church choir for many years. When I met him he had a mixed circle of friends from the local neighbourhood and they spent many happy hours hanging out on Farnhill moor. The circle was just beginning to break up as they were all in their late teens and early twenties and were starting to focus more on their careers, other interests, new friends and of course the opposite sex. Norman has never been a great decision maker and at the time we were getting to know each other, he was happy to follow the guidance of his Mum and Dad who had helped him to acquire an apprenticeship in Mechanical Engineering. He handed over most of his earnings to his Mum who chose most of his clothes, including as I found out later, the most grotesque underpants! He copied his parents' choice in fashion, entertainment and holidays and appears not to have gone through the rebellious adolescent phase.

In many ways Norman has remained the same, cautious of change and happy to let others make the decisions. He has continued to be a loyal friend and has become a relaxed and easy going Dad and a kind, gentle and faithful husband. Happy in his chosen career, Norman never wanted to join the rat race to the top, and so never sought promotion. A man who was clearly happy with his lot.

Shock horror then for his Mum and Dad when they met me! A town girl with a part time job at our local grammar school waiting for a place to train as a nurse, a training I never completed. Although I was shy in social situations, I was highly motivated and ambitious. In contrast to Norman's domestic tranquillity, I constantly challenged my parents, especially my Mum. She was a four foot ten blond bombshell who got away with wearing teenage clothes, loads of makeup, and lived life to the full. She probably frightened Norman's mother to death.

I think the relationship survived because Norman was happy to let me have my own way and I had plenty of ideas of what I wanted, selfish pig that I am. I have never had a problem making decisions, and do in fact thrive on it. I must have inherited my bossy nature from my Mum (but not her glamour), and I pretty much took control of my own life.

Basically, it seemed that Norman was transferring his dependent nature gradually from his parents to me, and this really set the tone for our eventual marriage. Even National Service did not change Norman's gentle nature and the dogmatic matrons and autocratic sisters didn't undermine my spirit.

So after a few ups and downs the families put their Sunday hats on along with their best manners, and we married in 1959. We put a £30 deposit towards a mortgage for a terraced family house and got on with it. Most of our furniture was second hand or borrowed, but gradually we replaced it with new stuff. By now Norman was well out of his apprenticeship and I, having abandoned a career in nursing, had a fairly well paid office job. I took tremendous pride in our new furniture and cleaned and polished like a maniac. I set a programme of Wednesday and Thursday evening as 'cleaning nights' and Norman reluctantly joined in, as long as he could listen to the radio. I'm not sure if this is where I began to develop my obsession with cleaning, but I had plenty of neighbours of the 'old school', anxious to teach me the rules. Steps were scrubbed and scoured, and washing could only be hung out to dry on Mondays, and only on the back street! I was most impressed.

We trotted happily along until I began to get the maternal urge. Norman definitely wanted children though he tended to think 'not just yet'. However, after trying for a couple of years, we had some investigations and discovered that we might have some trouble conceiving. After much discussion and debate we applied to adopt a baby boy – at that time boys were much more available than girls, and we were finally introduced to our son, Ian Mark, who we brought home on 23rd October 1962 aged 6 weeks. Ian had fair curly hair and blue eyes. He was a large cuddly boy and adorable from day one. On day two we discovered that he had a piercing scream that he could keep up all night if he wanted to. I don't think he was all that impressed with this doting but naïve and inexperienced couple.

A year later we moved to a lovely little semi-detached house with huge gardens at the back and front. It seemed a good time to think about adopting a second baby and we had a pleasant time being interviewed again by the Adoption Society, this time with Ian in tow. I remember the date well, March 10th 1964, Norman's 29th birthday. We were accepted onto the adoption waiting list and went home to prepare for baby number two. It was on the day, a couple of months later, when the social worker did her routine home visit that I first experienced the misery of morning sickness. Of course we had to cancel the adoption arrangements and Andrew arrived would you believe it, on 10th December 1964.

We felt then that our family was complete. Ian and Andrew were very different in nature. Ian outgoing, ready to deal with any challenges life threw his way and always into mischief. Andrew quieter, smiley, and as happy as the day is long. There was never a dull moment and we pottered along poor but content. We had lovely neighbours, all with young children who played happily together whilst we helped each other out through the small crises of family life.

Perhaps we were too complacent and only mildly surprised when I got the morning sickness again. Nicola was born in November 1966. It took quite a while to get used to saying 'she' instead of 'he'. Nicola was much like Ian in character, inquisitive and eager to be off and discover her world. We now had a truly fantastic little family, so I borrowed a posh hat and we trotted them all off to the Adoption Society to show them how clever and swanky we were. Our tiny semi became a bit stretched at the sides and we moved to a larger semi (with a smaller garden) high up out of town in a pretty village where we still live after 45 years. If we thought we were a staid established family of five, nature had one more surprise in store for us. He was called Julian and arrived in March 1970, a little early, a little unexpected, but welcome just the same. It took us a while to choose a name so he was called 'bonus' for the first couple of weeks. Julian, more like Andrew, was happy to play quietly by himself. Sunny in nature, he was by far the easiest to bring up.

By now our finances were severely stretched, and as Norman's pay was not brilliant, we puzzled over what to do. Although it was against Norman's cautious nature he applied for a job outside his area of expertise and moved into television design, which he came to love. I, meanwhile, entered the world of part-time youth work which I was able to do in the evenings while Norman cared for the children. Norman went on to enjoy his career for the next 20 years while I progressed in youth work through part-time training, and as the children grew older, I was able to go to college full time in order to qualify for full time youth work. After working as a leader in charge of several youth clubs, I applied to join the Education Welfare Service where I spent the next 12 years. I was able to side-track my youth work into tutoring on prospective leader courses which I could do in the evenings and at the weekend. We were now able financially, to put a little jam on our bread.

Chapter 2:

Alzheimer's - A Devastating Inheritance

Norman once told me how his maternal Granny was suddenly taken away to a mental institution in Mirfield because she had 'gone a bit funny' and couldn't remember who anyone was. Nobody gave a name to this illness but she never came home. Norman's Mum became a widow when she was only 51. His Dad Harold, developed lung cancer after working in a Blacksmiths shop, 30 years of smoking and a sedentary leisure life spent mainly on a bar stool. He died at the age of 52 while I was experiencing my first pregnancy. I remember us both throwing up together, he from radiation sickness. His Mum settled down to learning to live alone. She retired at 60yrs of age from her job in a knitting wool factory and was able to buy a mill house which she furnished in her own style. Norman and Raymond, his younger brother, did not visit her as often as I felt they should but I called quite regularly when the children were small.

As she reached her seventies, I noticed she began to repeat herself a lot. I began to notice mouldy food in her pantry and it became clear that she was neglecting herself to some extent. We managed to get her some day care at a local luncheon club but it became clear that her memory was failing badly. We returned from a holiday in 1998 to hear that she had had a nasty fall and was in hospital. Although she would have wished to return to her home she was assessed as having mild to moderate Alzheimer's disease and therefore unfit to live alone. After much searching we were able to find her a very nice residential home in familiar surroundings and she seemed quite happy. She used to say 'I am perfectly content, I have a room with a view'. She steadily deteriorated but continued to live there until she died in 2004 at the age of 91. Right to the end she was able to pursue her hobby of completing word puzzles.

This was my first hands on experience of Alzheimer's disease. Norman's Mum had not been easy to get along with in the early days of our relationship. She had very Victorian and dogmatic views and would not tolerate anyone else's opinion. She was very much the matriarch in the home and the boys very much toed the line. I have to remember that she lost her middle son, Stewart, in tragic circumstances when he was 3½ years old and acknowledge that this made her extremely protective towards her other sons. Norman was nine years older than Raymond, and I think a great comfort and support to her. Raymond who was only 18 months old when Stewart died, was a much more challenging boy. Right through the normal naughty behaviour of childhood and the rebellion of adolescence, he was much more complex than Norman. He left home at 18 years of age and joined the army without telling his parents, this caused them considerable heartache. Stewart had been the favoured child, with blonde curly hair and blue eyes, whilst the others were dark like their Mum. After Stewart died, their Mum seemed to lavish more affection on Norman and although she tried hard to treat both boys equally, it was obvious that Norman had first place in her affections. This was blatantly obvious to me when I got to know the family. I tried hard to befriend Raymond but he obviously had very mixed feelings about me and I was altogether too naive and inexperienced at the time to be able to respond in a positive way to Norman's Mum.

Harold had recieved an insurance pay out in 1954 after losing some fingers in an accident at work. He bought a second hand Vauxhall car which he and Norman raced each other to be qualified to drive. He also bought a washing machine, a vacuum cleaner and an Alba TV. Their Mum was very upset to find out later that the balance of the money was not in the bank, but had been frittered away by Harold who had acquired a whole host of new friends in the pub. She was obviously very bitter about this. Later, after Harold died, she became much more approachable and I got on with her quite well. I'm sure her having grandchildren had a lot to do with this.

Raymond had married, and he and Margaret produced five more grandchildren which gave her a total of nine. This made it easier to help her later when her memory failed and towards the end I think she was quite fond of me. I need to tell you more about our background later in the story.

Chapter 3:

Early Signs

As we became a more technological society the big computer gradually swallowed the need for draughtsmen and Norman twice became redundant. This did not do his confidence much good and he became depressed. It was around this time that I side tracked from my youth work and joined the local Education Welfare team. What with two jobs, and the challenge of my own teenage kids, I was probably too busy to notice how fed up Norman was. When I did realise he was a bit down, I tried to persuade him to look for work outside his own expertise and also to try to pick up some of his old interests. Although Norman had never been interested in sports or outdoor pursuits, he had enjoyed collecting tapes of his teenage taste in music. He had been a fan of Guy Mitchell, Frankie Lane and Doris Day and especially of the Big Band music of the 1940s. He was also quite good at making model aircrafts, an interest left over from his National Service when he worked on the Vulcan bomber. He enjoyed reading aircraft and train magazine, and also took an interest in novels by Andy McNab and Wilbur Smith. He was also very good at fixing problems with the car and mechanical tasks around the house. I tried to persuade him to pick up some of these interests again to fill his time and perhaps to spend a bit of time making an effort with the garden! I bought him a couple of model aircraft, but he seemed to struggle to make sense of the instructions. I noticed that when he painted them they didn't have the glossy precision of his earlier models. Perhaps even then he was struggling with brain function. Luckily he managed to get a job in the catering trade, packing pizzas. Although he found it physically taxing at first, he seemed to enjoy it as it carried no real responsibilities. The depression seemed to disappear and he was more amenable to meeting friends and going out for meals.

Norman retired on his 65th birthday. When asked what he intended to do in his retirement, his reply was always 'as little as possible', and that's exactly what he did! I could not persuade him to do maintenance tasks around the house or slap on a coat of paint. It seemed it was time for me to learn some new skills.

When he had been retired for about three months I noticed that he was beginning to put on weight. From a fairly physical job he was now sitting around watching day time TV. His waist line bulged and he needed a larger size in trousers. One memorable day I came home from work and he said he had seen an item on TV that suggested he might lose some weight if he ate a portion of fruit and a bowl of Special K (the cereal, not the drug!) for lunch instead of sandwiches. I said okay to Special K and bought him a box of the cereal. When I next cleaned the cupboards I noticed the box of Special K unopened. I asked Norman about his lunch diet and his reply quite alarmed me; "what a load of rubbish, I never asked for Special K, I've never seen a programme or advert about it. I don't know what you're talking about". After wondering if I was going crackers, I had to accept that there had been one or two similar incidents recently. He was certainly struggling to remember people's names, even his own grandchildren. He couldn't remember little things I had asked him to do while I was working. He was also less aware of his personal hygiene, forgetting to use deodorant, or clean his teeth. He became quite irritable when I mentioned this, so clearly at that point he was conscious of his lapses and was confused and embarrassed about them.

I was busy at work and still very much in denial that anything was seriously wrong. I just put it down to the ageing process. At the same time he sometimes refused to eat a certain food that he had previously enjoyed, such as bacon, saying he had never liked it. He suddenly demanded to wear a jumper when he had always refused before.

I had retired from Education Social Work and youth work at 60 years of age and got a part time job managing a sitting scheme for elderly and ill people, allowing their carer to take a short break. This was run by a local charity and financed by Social Services. Here, I came face to face with Alzheimer's disease on a daily basis, and although I took an academic interest and saw the distress experienced by the carers and family of sufferers, I never really appreciated the devastating results of living with someone who has this horrendous disease. There is little doubt that as we grow older, we begin to struggle with short term memory. How many times do we go upstairs and forget what we have gone for? Or need to make lists when we do our shopping? More embarrassing perhaps is when we meet an acquaintance and simply cannot remember their name. Someone once told me that this is because the memory is like a filing cabinet that gets pretty stuffed up by the time we reach middle age. A lot of what is in there is old stuff that we can't get rid of and there is no room for the more recent memories to be stored properly and things get mixed up. Simplistic perhaps, but easy to relate to, and you can extend it when material in the cabinet gets out of order so that we cannot remember which of two events happened first.

Because Alzheimer's disease is so much more in the news these days, people tend to panic when they notice they are becoming forgetful and approach their GP for help, when their memory loss is just part of the ageing process. Conversely, people who suffer from Alzheimer's do not realise that their memory is failing. When others mention a concern about their memory, they deny it, and often refuse to visit their GP.

I think the first time I heard the word Alzheimer's was, when a colleague in the youth service in the early eighties, told me her mother aged 60 had had to go into care because of this disease. I knew nothing about it and asked a GP I know, who described it at that time as pre-senile dementia. Now of course we know that is a particular form of dementia with distinctive characteristics, but it shows how recently the condition has been properly recognised. Although the signs and symptoms can lead to a diagnosis, and tests can rule out other conditions, I understand that an absolute diagnosis can only be made post mortem. Diagnosing Alzheimer's is one thing, though many people do have trouble getting a diagnosis, treating Alzheimer's is something else entirely and for people suffering today, there is very little that can be prescribed that can slow down and alleviate some of the symptoms of the disease and nothing so far that can claim to cure it.

As I was still working when Norman first had these memory lapses, I didn't have time to worry about it too much. He kept reasonably active at this point and I looked forward to a time when I could retire and we could perhaps spend days walking in the beautiful Yorkshire countryside, punctuated by pub lunches. I left my job as a care relief manager in 2001, having met a number of Alzheimer's sufferers and their carers, but knowing very little more about it. Norman's Mum was in her care home, and although she seemed settled and content, she was clearly becoming more and more confused and disorientated. For some reason, it disturbed Norman to visit her in the home, and I had to put a bit of pressure on him to make the effort. I was able to look after her practical needs, buying her clothes, toiletries etc. and managed her financial affairs, but I felt it was far more important for her to see Norman and his brother. At this time of course, we had to arrange for the disposal of Mum's home and possessions, and naturally Norman found this was very distressing. I assumed he was upset by the task of closing this chapter of his Mum's life, and I'm sure he was. However, it became obvious that he was simply not up to the task of form filling, contacting the council and service providers etc. At first I put this down to laziness, but looking back, I realise that he had been leaving the form filling tasks to me for quite some time, saying that he did not understand them.

Not long after we were both retired, we bought a 4th hand static caravan in the Lake District. The idea was for us to spend quiet weeks together up there and for the family to use it whenever they could. Nicola and Paul and their four children already had a caravan on the same site, so we shared lots of fun times together. It was lovely when other grand kids joined us and I have some wonderful memories of this time.

One thing about a caravan is that no matter how big it is, you can only spend a limited amount of time cleaning it. There was a very efficient laundrette on site and a well stocked shop. There were plenty of maintenance jobs like painting the decking and cutting the grass which kept Norman busy, and he seemed to quite enjoy these tasks, much more than he would have done at home. We spent many hours walking in this beautiful area and sampling the fare of the many charming tea shops. Having nine Grandchildren meant that we were always kept occupied when they came. I particularly enjoyed midnight walks through the wood, frightening each other to death with ghost stories. Looking back this was the happiest part of our retirement. We were always pleased to come home to the central heating in the winter, but soon after Christmas we would start looking forward to going to the caravan again.

For the past 20 years, we have spent our main holiday in Goa. Everybody has a favourite place and the attractions of Goa, especially in the winter, were the warmth, the laid back atmosphere, the fantastic food and the truly lovely people. Of course like anywhere else, there have been many changes as the resorts have developed, not all of them for the better. However the principal attractions, plus the beautiful countryside and fantastic beaches have taken us back year after year.

Whilst due to Norman's illness, holidays either in the caravan or Goa are no longer possible, I have some wonderful memories to comfort me. Sadly for Norman, he had only a vague recollection of Goa and cannot remember the caravan at all. I wonder if I would be brave enough to go back to Goa alone. I would certainly like to, we will have to see!

It was during times away from home that I began to notice more acutely Norman's difficulties when in unfamiliar surroundings. In the early days at the caravan he was still driving, and although his driving skills seemed alright, he sometimes lost his sense of direction and we often took the scenic route through pretty villages. He was often disorientated for the first couple of days especially through the night when he could not find the bathroom.

It's strange how at the time I simply did not worry about any of this. We had lots of laughs about the funny mistakes he made and we just put it all down to old age creeping up. I must admit, I tried to get him to use little tricks to try to nudge his memory such as working through the alphabet when trying to remember someone's name, but he thought I was exaggerating the problem. Although his Mum by this time had deteriorated considerably, she still had some success in following word search puzzles which she had been doing for years. Norman had no real interest in this kind of puzzle, but at one time he had enjoyed doing jigsaw puzzles. I bought a couple to see if it would stimulate his brain, one of steam engines which he had always had an interest in, and one of a Monet painting he used to like. For a while he persevered with these with the family joining in when they could, but it soon became clear that he was never going to be able to complete them and he became frustrated and gave up trying. He no longer wanted to join in games like Monopoly and Scrabble which we played in the cooler evenings in the caravan. Again, I put it down to old age and laziness. At that time, when discussing Mum's illness, I had been assured that it was extremely unlikely that there was a gene connection in Alzheimer's and the fact that his Mum had the illness and his memory was poor, was just a coincidence.

It was around this time that Raymond, Norman's brother, had a series of mini strokes. This was followed by a major stroke which left him with limited mobility and some mental impairment. He was ill in hospital for many weeks, and Margaret, his wife, had to prepare herself for a very different lifestyle when he came home. She found it very hard to adjust at first but was able to arrange respite breaks which made an enormous difference. Raymond has not deteriorated much since his stroke and his mental ability remains about the same. This is probably one of the differences between vascular dementia and Alzheimer's. Further information about the different forms of dementia can be found in the increasing number of books on the subject, or from the Alzheimer's Society. Norman managed to visit

Raymond from time to time to pass on railway magazines which was an interest they both shared. Because of the nine year age difference, the brothers did not have a great deal in common. Whilst Norman completed two years National Service, he could not match Raymond's long army career which took him all over Europe where he acquired many new friends and interests.

It was after I finally retired that I made my mind up to improve our lifestyle health-wise. Now that I had more time, it was easier to cook more home made meals and to spend hours chopping vegetables and preparing delicious salads. I haven't eaten meat since 1991, but Norman is a confirmed carnivore and has an excellent appetite. He still enjoys a wide range of foods and never refuses second helpings. I had taken up walking and swimming and set myself a goal of 25,000 miles on foot and 1000 miles in the water before my 75th birthday. I am still on target! Try as I might, I could not persuade Norman to join me in these activities. He did walk more when we were at the caravan or on holiday, but usually under sufferance. His improved diet must have worked where the Special K never got started. By the time he was 70 in 2005, Norman had a nice slim figure. Physically, he has kept in very good health apart from some problems with his blood pressure. Norman has always been interested in current affairs, especially at a local level, and has enjoyed regional and national news on TV. He collected the local paper, The Telegraph and Argus, each day from a nearby shop and used to read it cover to cover, apart from the sports pages which he ignored. He enjoyed reading bits out to me and would enjoy discussions over a cup of coffee. I began to notice that he was reading the same pieces out again after we had had the discussion. At first I mentioned it, but he was obviously embarrassed, so I learned to be more sensitive and to go along with having the discussion again. It was at this point that other forms of repetitive behaviour began to appear. We had laughed together when his Mum had kept telling us the same tale over and over, but I didn't find it at all funny when Norman started to do it. It is strange that at that time, I still did not seriously consider that Norman might be in the early stages of Alzheimer's disease. His Mum's condition was so severe by now, that the changes in Norman seemed very mild. As well as that, when you live with someone day in day out, you do not notice the subtle changes in their behaviour.

Norman's Mum celebrated her 91st birthday on 7th May 2004. We came back from the caravan to visit her in her care home, to take her present and share her cake. Less than 2 days later, she had a sudden stroke and died instantly. When she was admitted into care she was quite lucid, was able to hold a reasonably sensible conversation, and still enjoyed reading, word puzzles and TV. Her deterioration seemed very gradual until a few months before she died. From then on, she was unable to recognise us, and could not form words anymore. She was certainly unaware that Norman was showing signs of having Alzheimer's disease.

After Mum died, we were able to spend longer periods at the caravan. Although it was in fantastic condition, there was a strict site code that caravans had to be removed or replaced after they were fifteen years old. After much discussion we decided to share a much newer

24

model with Rachel and Julian which we purchased in June 2004. Norman and I certainly got more use out of it than the family did as they were restricted to weekends and holiday periods. Gradually, as the grandchildren grew older, they developed other interests and did not enjoy trips to the caravan as much. In 2007 we decided it was time to move on, and sold the caravan to a lovely couple who we have kept in contact with. I have regrets to this day, but am comforted by the many happy memories of those years. It is so sad that Norman cannot recall any of this period and is unable to recognise the many photographs we took.

We had both wanted to visit Australia and New Zealand for quite some time and so, instead of putting money from the sale of the caravan to more practical use, we decided to blow it on the holiday of a lifetime. By now Norman was unable to make clear decisions about financial matters, so the decision to take the holiday was largely mine. How glad I am that we went. I had subconsciously realised that our holidays together were numbered as Norman's confusion increased, and that if we were going to go for it, it was now or never. Luckily we had friends, another couple our age, going on the same tour, so I didn't feel entirely alone with any problems I might have to face whilst we were away from home.

Although the holiday lived up to my expectations in every way, there was enough concern about Norman's mental health to make me realise that once we were home, I needed to seek some help. There are certainly however, some lighter and humorous moments from our holiday. The first stage of the holiday was a night at a

Travelodge near Heathrow. To save bother, I had bought Norman a Micky Mouse t-shirt and shorts to sleep in for £2.50 which I intended to throw away the next day, but somehow forgot. Our first flight was to Singapore where we met the rest of our tour party. We were all pretty exhausted and as our rooms were not ready, we were offered a trip to the Changi Prisoner of War museum. Norman insisted he had been there before and complained that some of the exhibits had been moved. I had to take him out to avoid a scene! We were relieved to eventually get to bed and to save searching suitcases, I gave Norman the Micky Mouse nightwear. During the night, I was disturbed by a heavy knocking at the door, and found Norman out there desperately looking for a toilet. Even though I had left the light on in the bathroom he was too disorientated to find it. I hoped he hadn't disturbed anyone and settled him down to sleep. A couple of hours later, I woke suddenly to realise he was not in the room or the bathroom. I was absolutely panic stricken because we were on the 9th floor with only a dozen or so rooms. The lift would take him to the lobby but he would be unable to get back without the room card to operate the ascending lift. This was a security measure. I simply stood in the bedroom doorway for ages wondering what to do. Eventually he re-appeared with his shorts in tatters. I do not know where he had been, but he told me he had weed in a fire bucket! We managed to get about another hours sleep and dressed groggily to go and find some breakfast. The other members of our group asked us if we had seen an elderly gentleman wondering around during the night with tattered shorts! It wasn't until the very end of the holiday that I felt confident enough to confess. Obviously they were highly amused but they were aware of Norman's problems by then, and were sensitive enough to be very sympathetic towards him.

During the holiday, we moved from country to country and hotel to hotel, probably about twelve hotels in total. I frequently asked Norman if he knew where he was but he couldn't even remember the name of the country, let alone the hotel. I kept a close eye on him and made sure that his name and details were always in his pocket.

The worst incident was at Sydney airport towards the end of the holiday when we were flying to Bangkok. He was taken aside by security staff to 'answer a few questions'. I pointed out that he had a memory problem but was not allowed to accompany him. They took him behind a curtain and I could hear what was being said. They asked him where he was travelling to and he said he did not know. They asked him to try hard to remember, and he said "Taiwan". After this, I had had enough, and barged through the curtain to rescue him. Luckily they were quite sympathetic and assured me that he had not been singled out, and that it was just a random check. In spite of all these hitches, Norman really enjoyed his holiday. We saw some of the most beautiful sights on earth as well as some of the seven wonders. We had really excellent guides who gave lots of help and advice, and many extras that weren't included in the holiday itinerary. Best of all, we were with a fantastic group of people who helped to make sure we enjoyed every minute.

It was while we were away that I realised how disorientating being in unfamiliar surrounding can be to a person who has memory problems. Just finding a bathroom in the middle of the night can be a major worry. So I developed a knack of waking up when Norman stirred (rather like you do when a baby needs feeding in the night). I was able to escort him to the loo and safely back to bed. This ability stood me in good stead, especially more recently when he couldn't find his way around even at home.

Shortly after our return from our trip to Australia, I went to see the GP about Norman. I explained his refusal to accept there was anything wrong, and that he saw no reason to talk to his doctor. Norman did take medication for high blood pressure, and for prostate problems, so it was easy for the doctor to say that he needed a review anyway. He suggested conducting a small memory test while he was in the surgery and advised me to accompany him. It felt a bit like deceit, so in the end I told Norman that he would be having a memory test due to my concerns. He grumbled a bit but was quite co-operative with the GP. It was patently obvious, even from this very simple test, that Norman had much more than a bad memory. The doctor pointed out that it was necessary to get a proper diagnosis before he could suggest a way forward, and he referred him to the Bradford Memory Assessment Centre.

His first appointment was in September 2008. We did not know what to expect from the interview and Norman was reluctant to go, still insisting that his memory was fine. We were seen by the Consultant Psychiatrist who conducted a rather more formal memory test. This involved the doctor saying three words; ball, watch and pen, then asking Norman to keep them in mind. He went on to other tests such as asking Norman to spell words backwards, some simple facts around politicians and the royal family, and asking him to copy some shapes. The doctor kept returning to the three words he had asked Norman to remember. There were other questions all designed to gauge just how far Norman's memory was failing. Although the tests seemed a bit crude, it is difficult to think of a more scientific way of testing someone's memory.

Afterwards, the doctor told us that Norman had a score of 24 on the test. Anyone with a score below 30 is considered to have some level of dementia. Norman was diagnosed as having mild Alzheimer's disease subject to ruling out other forms of dementia. We were told that he was suitable for taking part in a drug trial which was commencing shortly. We were given some information to take away so we could consider whether this was what Norman wanted to do. This was a double blind test which was being tested worldwide. We would not know whether Norman was being given a full dose of the drug, a small dose, or a placebo. A full medical check including blood and urine tests would be given plus regular follow ups and he would need to have a brain scan to rule out other forms of dementia such as vascular incidents or a tumour. He would be able to continue with his normal medication for high blood pressure and benign prostate problems, but would not be able to take any drugs connected with memory loss such as Aricept. By this time Norman was not able to take part in any serious discussion about his health, so it was mostly down to me to decide. Of course I discussed it with my family. My daughter Nicola who is a nurse was not entirely happy with the idea of introducing strange drugs to her Dad. The boys had mixed feelings, especially as there was little else on offer. In the end we decided to go for it, especially because his health would be carefully monitored whilst he was taking the drug.

So, he had a brain scan which revealed no evidence of vascular problems or a tumour, and we went back to the Memory Assessment Centre to commence his first dose. The trial was for six months, and this was the final phase of the trial. Every month or so after the initial dose, we were taken by taxi to the centre to enable Norman to have his health check, and also to collect a fresh supply of the medication. At these sessions, both Norman and I were interviewed separately to check if there were any changes in Norman's memory or behaviour. Apparently it is quite common in these trials for there to be some placebo effect in the early stages, simply because the person knows they are having some treatment. Norman's memory test score increased to 26 in the first month of the trial and then hovered around 24-22 for the next five months.

At the end of the six month period, we were offered a further six months continuous period, this time knowing that Norman would be taking a full dose of the drug. As there had been no side effects so far, we agreed to this. He continued to take his medication for four months when they told us that the original trial had failed to show any difference between those who were taking either dose of the drug, and those who were taking the placebo. He was given the option of continuing to take the doses if he wanted to, but now he was becoming unsettled by the journey and the blood tests etc. His mental state did seem to have deteriorated a bit so the clinic doctor suggested asking our GP to prescribe Aricept (Doneprezil). This was not as straight forward as it appears as there are directions to GPs from National Institute for Clinical Excellence (N.I.C.E.) about prescribing these very expensive drugs on the NHS. However, because this had been rubber stamped by the Consultant at the clinic, we were able to obtain the prescription. Although we knew Aricept was not a cure for Alzheimer's, we were hoping that it would slow down the process. We have kept in touch with the memory centre who often offer the opportunity for further trials.

Norman has never had a good memory for names, but it upset me a little to realise that he could not remember the names of his own grandchildren. Admittedly, nine is quite a lot of names to remember. I suppose they were growing at such a rate that he sometimes didn't even recognise them and Lucy was quite put out when he walked passed her at the bus stop without knowing who she was. It was more understandable that he wouldn't remember the four grandchildren in Scotland and the two in Cheshire as he saw them less often, but the three in the same street he saw most days.

It was also around this time that he began to refer to 'the lads'. 'Are the lads upstairs?', 'have the lads had their tea?', 'I'd better look for the lads'. I asked if he was referring to Ian, Andrew and Julian, our sons, or Daniel, Charlie, Luke, Adam, Callan and William, our grandsons, but he always said 'no, no, no, *the* lads!' Although Aricept did seem to make him more alert, he appeared to suffer from quite a few delusions. He would ask to go home, even though he was at home, and seemed puzzled when I explained this. He would see mice or other animals in the house and often asked where our cat was. We've never owned a cat, but I believe he had one as a child. He would sometimes say he was going to look for Mary, even though I was there with him. His mother was also called Mary, so I checked to see if he meant her, and he said 'No, I mean my wife'. He could get angry very easily during this stage. Although Norman has never been aggressive, he certainly became more excitable at this stage. In order to emphasise a point, he would bang his hands down quite heavily on my shoulders, which are a bit delicate anyway. He also became very agitated if I tried to take anything from him, such as his shaver, which he tried to stuff in his pocket.

The next phase of the illness to affect Norman was definitely most trying for me. He became very clinging, and would not let me out of his sight. I have always enjoyed walking and still tried to have at least one hour's walk each day. As Norman preferred to be more sedentary, I enjoyed this space to myself. Suddenly, this became impossible. He insisted on coming with me, even though he couldn't keep up with my normal pace or go the full distance. So the walks became slower, shorter, and less pleasurable for me as he grumbled the whole time. I managed to get hold of some literature dealing with this kind of behaviour but did not find it very helpful as it looked at the problem from the point of view of the person with Alzheimer's. Understanding why people behave as they do helps you to empathise, but in the clinging situation, all I wanted was help to make it stop happening. Trying to reason with Norman did not help because he no longer had any insight into his behaviour. He interpreted the clinging as being loving and needing me by his side every moment. It may have been at this time that I began to try to detach myself from the emotional burden of caring for Norman. I felt I was being swallowed up by his illness, and that my every waking moment was affected by it.

Because I have always been fiercely independent, I tried not to grumble too much to my family. When I did have a bit of a moan, I think they thought I was exaggerating somewhat. Perhaps they didn't want to look closely at the implications of Norman's illness.

In June 2010, I was admitted to hospital for surgery to repair a prolapsed uterus and needed to stay in for four nights. Julian, who lived nearby, agreed to sleep over on these nights to make sure his Dad got to bed alright, and was up and about before Julian left for work. Norman simply could not understand why I needed to be in hospital and was bewildered by this arrangement. However, it seemed to work alright from my point of view, and I was surprised when Julian and Rachel asked me to pop into their house for a chat about Dad when I came home. Clearly, prior to sleeping over for those four nights, Julian had no idea of the extent of Norman's illness. He had found him extremely unco-operative and self absorbed. He could not persuade Norman to have a proper wash or bath, or care for his clothing. Neither was he sure that his Dad ate adequately during the day. Of course Julian and Rachel passed on their concerns to the rest of the family, and suddenly I had a support system. I have to confess, I enjoyed being in hospital, and when told I had to stay a fourth night, I told them I would stay a month if they liked! Perhaps I had not realised how much caring for Norman was taking out of me, and how much I needed a break.

By this time I had contacted the Carers' Resource. I knew of them because of my previous job as a short-break care provider, and I felt that they were my first professional line of support as a carer. I was allocated a support worker who came to see us both. She was able to provide information and advice on a variety of issues, and made sure we were claiming any financial entitlement. More importantly, Sarah was able to give me some objective emotional support, and stayed in contact with me throughout.

Looking back, I realise I should have asked for help much sooner. There was quite a bit of arrogance in my assertion that I could manage. I was clear that I was capable of caring for Norman come what may, and I resisted what I termed outside interference.

Chapter 4:

My OCD Personality

To understand how I initially dealt with Norman's problems, you need to know a little more of my history. My parents met through the enjoyment of ballroom dancing and after a short romance were married in 1934. They were a working class couple who worked hard during the day, and lived it up in the evenings and weekends. They had a crowd of like-minded mates and thought these halcyon days would last forever. So perhaps it was as well that I did not arrive until 1938. Neither of them had the slightest idea about parenthood or had any intention of giving up the good life. I'm sure they loved me, but they had no idea what to do with me. They both needed to work to fund their leisure habits so I had a series of baby minders, some good, some bad. This is probably where I learned to be self reliant and to use whatever it took to get what I wanted. As the country went to war in 1939, my Dad was enlisted in the Duke of Wellington's regiment. He was based in Selby for a period, but when he sensed that moving abroad to the war zone was imminent, he went Absent without Leave (A.W.O.L.). Because of problems with child minding, he came home and took me with him. I was only about 3 but I remember sharing a draughty room with him above a jewellers shop in Blackpool. My Dad had taught himself to repair clocks and watches so he was able to earn a bit of money through the jeweller. I remember spending a lot of time going round and round on Fairyland along the golden mile – all for three-pence. I'm not sure how long we were away for, or if he was punished for going A.W.O.L, but he never went back to the army. He came back home to unemployment and earned what he could by mending clocks and watches, at first at home, and then later he rented a shop. This took care of child minding problems and I spent many hours polishing gem stones and learning to identify a balance staff or a hair spring. I earned a bit of pocket money by finding tiny parts that he had dropped on the floor – my eyes were sharper than my Dad's. At a penny a find, I did quite well.

On a lovely warm day in June 1943, I went home to find I had acquired a baby brother. I was truly amazed as nobody had consulted me about this! I was now attending school but the baby care problems started all over again with my brother David. During the war, it was easy for my Mother to get work in munitions and she enjoyed this routine work as it gave her lots of time to chat with her colleagues. Because she was doing 'war work', David was accepted at a day nursery where she only had to pay a shilling a day. David has fond memories of his days at the Woodbine nursery.

It was when David started school at the age of 4 years that the problems began for me. I had to get him to school as my parents both left the house before us. I had to collect him after school and take him home, start the tea and set the fire. It was very difficult to get him to do what I told him so I was a bit heavy handed with him. At times I dreaded him growing bigger than me and getting his own back. It was even worse in the evenings as our parents always went out to follow their leisure pursuits, mainly in a pub or working men's club. I had often been left alone as a toddler while my Mum worked as a bar maid and my Dad was in the army so I was quite used to this. Looking after David was something else as he was a total monkey. It was very difficult to get him to go to bed and to get him to settle when he got there. On two occasions he managed to set fire to the bed. Of course my parents were horrified about this and it was easier for them to blame me than to take responsibility for their own neglect. I thought the punishment was totally unjustified, but I was nine years old and helpless to do much about it. Another problem was that we were both neglected physically and were often sent to school unwashed and in dirty clothes. It didn't seem to bother David much but I was acutely aware that other girls didn't want to be friends with me.

When I was 11 years old I passed what was then called 'the scholarship' to gain a place at the local grammar school. Both my parents refused to allow me to take my place, arguing that I would get ideas above my station and would become a 'snob' and talk 'posh'. My father in particular was rather Victorian and felt that a grammar school was no place for girls. There was good money to be earned in the textile industry and anyway, girls only got married. It was at this stage in my life that I realised it was now or never. I was completely rebellious and marched round to my grandparents and aunts and uncles to drum up some support. Whilst they were sympathetic, they were all a bit daunted by my mum and dad, and didn't want to get involved. I wrote a letter to the Education Officer, and pushed it through the letter box of the local office. I threatened to sit on the office steps night and day until they answered it. I never knew what happened about that letter, but I was told quietly by my Mum that she had persuaded my Dad to let me go to the grammar school. This episode set the theme for my teenage years. Somewhere along the line I realised that my destiny was pretty much in my own hands and that from the chaotic parenting I had received, there were some useful assets. Certainly I had acquired quite a few life skills on domestic lines. The family shopping was usually my responsibility, and although a pretty useless cook, I was better at it than my parents. As I had had to take a lot of responsibility for the care of my brother, I must have learned some parenting skills. We were given a great deal of freedom compared with our mates and became quite streetwise. David has a much more sunny and gentle nature than I and he seemed to sail through without too much trauma. I had to fight a bit harder to survive, but luckily I have a strong sense of responsibility which protected David somewhat and kept me from going off the rails. I never had any desire to smoke or drink alcohol and because I was strong willed and bossy, I never had any problem saying no to anything I didn't want to do.

By the time I was 19 years old and was already involved with Norman, I was extremely independent and well able to live on my own. My mother had a habit of moving to Margate with some theatrical friends every summer, leaving her domestic and maternal responsibilities with me. My Dad was happy to go to work during the day and to the pub during the evening. This all came to a head when one summer I managed to get David into a school camp and he was sent home half way through the three week holiday with Asian flu. He became very ill indeed and I was obliged to stay away from work to care for him. I brought his bed downstairs near the fire as he was so cold and I had to change him every couple of hours. It was a major job to get fluids into him. The GP gave me some advice over the phone but could not call in due to his heavy workload caused by the Asian flu outbreak. It was two weeks before I could persuade David to eat anything and he asked for tomato soup. I went across to the local Co-op to get a tin, and could not believe that he was up and dressed and outside when I returned. Unexpectedly my Mum had returned from Margate and went berserk when she found him in bed downstairs. It didn't improve matters when she found out I had lost two weeks wages to care for him and she was furious that we had not warned her not to come home just yet as she didn't want to catch the Asian flu! I was equally furious and within 24 hours found myself a flat in Bradford close to where I worked. I borrowed some money from friends to get me going and never looked back. I learned to cook cheap and healthy meals and invested in a bucket, scrubbing brush and bleach etc. Within a month my little flat was spotless and comfortable and within two months I had repaid all the money I had borrowed.

Whilst I had some traumatic experiences at the time, I have never been bitter about the quality of my childhood. My parents were simply victims of their own upbringing and the challenges they had to face such as struggling with a war and unemployment. They did what many other people did at that time and put their own needs before those of their children. They certainly did not mean any harm, but we were just children and our interests, friends and aspirations were of no importance to them. Much later when they became grandparents, they were both able to look back and accept the mistakes they had made. They were both loving and caring grandparents and were rewarded with many happy hours spent enjoying the love and joy that they brought as grandma and grandad. This perhaps explains to some extent why I am as I am. My family tell me that I have Obsessive Compulsory Disorder (O.C.D.). Naturally I disagree with that analysis, who wouldn't! When I was first married, it was a virtue to have a clean and tidy home. You were expected to scrub the kitchen floor each day. Mansion polish not diamonds brought the sparkle that was a girls' best friend. A washing line of whiter than white fresh clean linen was something to be proud of as was a freshly scoured back step. Cooking, not kissing, was what made you a wife to be proud of, and if you could accomplish all this whilst going out to work, then you were considered a success by all the critical ladies of the neighbourhood.

At that time, my understanding was that someone who was O.C.D. was a person who was constantly checking that they had switched the light out, or turned the tap off. They were victims of a compulsion that drove them to repetitive actions in a vain attempt to assure themselves that all was well. It was regarded as an illness, and you saw a shrink and got fixed. Simplistic perhaps but nothing to do with old fashioned standards and pride in one's home.

The changing role of women in western society has had huge implications on the domestic scene. Machines do much of the hard graft, whilst the women these appliances replaced contribute to the workforce and the economy. The home is often empty for much of the day and meals are taken away from the home and therefore there is less domestic toil. What chores are done, are often shared by family members and the accent is more on leisure pursuits once the working day is over. Tidiness and even cleanliness is no longer a virtue, instead it is considered something of a vice. A home that looks 'lived in' is the order of the day and some children's bedrooms often look more like something has died in them.!

I have absolutely no quarrel with this. Society has moved with the times and it is important that a family enjoys the benefit of modern living and spend more time enjoying life together rather than washing curtains and cleaning the car. But for me, because of the chaos of my childhood home, because my home is my place of safety, because of pride, and because of who I am, I would delay fun time until all the jobs are done. It is not just domestic chores that are influenced by this sense of orderliness. If I receive a letter, I immediately answer it, If I get a bill, I pay it, if I have a complaint, I am straight on the phone, and if I have a problem, I solve it. If I can't solve it, then it is someone else's problem.

So, whether you want to call this O.C.D, being well organised, or just plain crackers, that is how I am. I don't particularly want to change my behaviour and it has never affected how I brought up my children. But it does not make me the ideal person to care for someone who has Alzheimer's disease. Whilst Norman is usually more comfortable in a routine, some aspects of his behaviour increasingly challenge my orderliness. Whilst I understand what is happening to him, it does not make me happier about it. As he gradually loses control of his movements and his finesse inevitably things get broken, soiled and stained. In many ways, his behaviour is like that of a clumsy toddler, but of course a toddler will gradually learn to modify his behaviour. A person suffering from Alzheimer's disease is unable to learn by experience, neither are they able to learn any new skills to help them to cope.

Having brought up four children through all the learning experiences of the growth years, it is quite daunting to think I have to do this again in reverse. Add to that the fact that I am in my seventies, not twenties, plus my need to be in control, it is hardly surprising that I feel inadequate faced with the task of caring for Norman. Worst of all is knowing that his condition can only deteriorate. 'Where has my husband gone?' I ask myself. I want to share my concerns and my unhappiness with him but he simply cannot even understand he has an illness, let alone how I feel about it. I do so envy other couples I come across where the carer appears to be so laid back and able to deal with all the trials and day to day demands. Why can't I be more like that?

Whilst some aspects of Norman's behaviour would be acceptable to a person who is not too concerned about routine and knowing where everything is, I find it increasingly trying. Hiding things is a common feature of Alzheimer's disease and it is constantly frustrating and time consuming searching for everyday objects and eventually finding them in the most bizarre places. Some things are so well hidden that I am afraid they stay lost! No carer escapes the agony of realising that a loved one is gradually losing the ability to care for themselves. When that loved one begins to lose factors of their personality which make them unique, who they are, there is a deep sense of loss and grief. The dynamics of the relationship shift as the affected person becomes more dependant. The pressure of responsibility on the carer increases to the point where the carer's lifestyle is inhibited by having to consider the sufferer's needs before their own. Where the carer is the spouse, there is no longer a sense of partnership and the comfort of sharing decisions, problems, sadness and joy is lost forever. The challenge faced by carers as the disease progresses affects their physical, mental and emotional well being. A lot depends on the personality of the carer and I am very conscious that the way I developed through my upbringing has made me an independent, practical and routine minded person. I feel safe and in control whenever my life is well ordered, but quite threatened when this sense of security is assailed. This is why caring for someone whose illness made it impossible for me to be practical, organised and precise is especially challenging and why I feel something of a failure in the way I have looked after Norman. I have not met all his needs by any means. After he lost the ability to choose what he would like to eat, I have made sure he has eaten a well balanced and healthy diet. I have made sure his hygiene needs were met, especially as he became incontinent, and even though he resisted my help at times. His clothes and shoes have been well cared for, his hair cut and his nails trimmed. All his health needs have been followed up and medical and dental appointments kept. I have encouraged him to take regular exercise, perhaps too much, and tried to make sure we still meet friends and family to maintain his social life. What I have not done, is to make allowances for his failing skills and to let him act spontaneously and make a mess if he wants to. If Norman finds he cannot complete a task, he loses patience and takes it out on what he is trying to do. When he cannot tie his shoe laces, he will rip them out of the shoes. If he can't locate something in a drawer, he will throw everything onto the floor. He is increasingly stubborn and resistant to suggestions, and can become quite aggressive if I try to take something from him. Where, I wonder, is my mild mannered, easy going husband?

Christmas time, 2008

Our Ruby Wedding, 1999

Norman's 70th birthday party in Goa, March 2005

(L-R) Ian, Julian, Nicola and Andrew at our Golden Wedding party, April 2009

Alice Springs Australia, ANZAC Day, April 2008

A rare picture of all nine grandchildren together

Up close with Nicola, April 2009

50 happy years, April 2009

Chapter 5:

Getting Help

In April 2011, we went with Julian and Rachel and their three children to stay with Nicola in Scotland. To make it as easy as possible for Norman, he travelled with Julian in the front of the car, while Rachel, Lucy and Charlie sat in the back seat. Daniel and I travelled by train, and I must admit, it was a real break for me to chat with Daniel, who at 15, was far more able to hold an adult conversation than Norman now was. Of course, the car arrived before the train did, and Norman became quite distressed, wondering where I was. This set the tone for the few days we were there as he absolutely refused to let me out of his sight. If I was helping in the kitchen, he wanted to stand next to me. He became very angry if I suggested going for a walk with Nicola and Rachel, yet refused to come with us. Sadly, he no longer recognised Nicola's children, who admittedly had grown considerably since we last saw them. He appeared agitated and disorientated. I don't think he really knew where he was or who all these people were, and he was irritable and snappy. I think everyone was relieved when it was time to come home, not least myself, and at least I was able to relax on the train journey back with Daniel. It was after this break that I finally realised I was going to have to try and get some help. The family had been saying for ages that I needed to try and arrange some care for Norman so that I could have some space for myself.

Norman had been taking Aricept for several months and I had noticed that he was certainly more alert and aware. However, over a period of time, he became more stubborn and aggressive and as I had noticed that this could be a side effect of the Aricept on the patient information leaflet, I mentioned it on our next visit to the Memory Assessment Centre. The result of Norman's cognitive test had dropped to 17, and they suggested that they should contact our GP with a view to trying a different drug, Exelon (Rivastigimine) to see if this was of more benefit.

We visited the GP who prescribed the Exelon, and suggested I should organise some day care for Norman. He advised me to contact Social Services. Simple and straightforward you would think! Unfortunately it was not, and so I include this rather lengthy saga in the hope that other carers can avoid the resistance and obstacles I had to face.

Having found the correct department (Adult Services), I introduced Norman and myself and asked if we could apply for day-care. The assistant advised me that this had to be done by the Bradford office, but she very kindly dialled the number for me so that I could speak to the correct department. Having explained my needs to the lady in Bradford, I was advised that the Social Services day-care was not the best solution to my problem. She said that day-care was very expensive, and that Norman was not in 'the system'. She offered to send me a list of local voluntary groups which might be able to provide some suitable day-care, and in my innocence, I accepted this offer.

A comprehensive list of church, leisure interest, political and other groups promptly arrived, and we sat down to consider what might suit Norman. Eventually, we decided to try an over 50's group at a fairly local church. This, the programme said, was held on a Wednesday afternoon between 2pm-4pm. There was a phone number to contact, and a very pleasant lady told me that we would be very welcome. She said there was a variety of speakers and events, followed by tea and a raffle. This sounded quite inviting, so we set off with the idea that I might accompany Norman a few times and subsequently drop him off for the session and pick him up at the end. We had a pleasant afternoon listening to well known poetry. The tea was lovely, and we won two packets of biscuits in the raffle. The trouble was that the event finished at 3.15pm. When I enquired about this, I was told that the finishing time varied a lot according to what was on the programme. This made my idea of getting a break away from Norman impractical, and although we did attend a couple more sessions, it did not meet my needs.

As I felt I needed something more formal than this, I contacted the Bradford Social Services office to request an assessment for local authority day-care. It was a case of 'leave a message' and after several attempts I did just that. Several days later, I had a return call from a male social worker. I explained that I was becoming quite worn out and distressed looking after Norman, and that my GP had suggested day-care. He asked what I wanted to use the break for, and I told him I enjoyed walking, and felt very nervous of leaving Norman alone at home for even a short while. He asked me what was the worst thing that could happen whilst I was out, and I replied that if Norman decided to make toast or something, he could set the place on fire. His reply was that I could get some efficient smoke alarms, and that I should see a counsellor about my feelings of inadequacy. There was obviously no point in continuing the conversation, and I hung up the phone in distress and despair, although I did think the idea of counselling had some merit. I look back and wonder why I allowed myself to be such a wimp. It may be that I resented having to ask for help in the first place, and was ambivalent about day-care anyway. Norman certainly didn't want to go to what I described as a social club. He didn't want to go anywhere unless I was with him. I know I had allowed my independence to overrule common sense, and should have been looking for day-care or even respite breaks much earlier. Because I had carried on to the point of exhaustion, I had lost something of my confidence and assertiveness. There was also a strong sense of duty – the bit about 'in sickness and in health' that made me feel I should be able to carry on whatever happened. This all seems ridiculous and martyrish now, but there's many a carer who has shared these feelings.

We needed to return to the GP to see how Norman was getting on with the Exelon, so I described my experience with Social Services and asked the Doctor to contact them on our behalf. Lo and behold, we had an appointment for an assessment of Norman's needs within three days, and within another two weeks, he was offered one day a week day-care. He was able to choose between 2 day centres; one bright and modern, one homely and cosy. I thought he would resist both, but to my surprise, after looking around, he chose the modern one.

It was around this time that Norman began to experience fainting attacks. He had had one previously at home when getting out of bed and his blood pressure had plummeted. He had been on three different tablets to control high blood pressure, so the Doctor discontinued one of these medications, and he seemed to be alright.However he began to have these fainting attacks again. The second time it happened he was in the Post Office and fell against a glass cabinet causing a head injury. An ambulance was called and the paramedics were concerned about his heart. He was taken to the local Airedale Hospital with the sirens screaming. Eventually his heart recovered, his head injury was dealt with and he was allowed home. We decided as a family then that Norman could not go far alone. In order that he could get some exercise I let him walk to the local paper shop, even though he was no longer able to really read the paper. He would also set off on short walks with me returning by a short-cut, if I wanted to continue my walk.

It was around this time that Norman was referred by his G.P. to the Consultant Psychiatrist for the elderly, I was expecting an appointment through the post when this gentleman arrived on my doorstep one Monday morning, unannounced. He explained that calling at the home like this gave him much better opportunity to see how the patient was coping. From my point of view he called at a good time. Norman was sitting in the conservatory with a cup of coffee, looking at the newspaper, and I was in the kitchen preparing a very healthy lunch. The house was clean and tidy and all was peaceful. The consultant asked Norman some questions intended to give him some idea of the level of Norman's dementia. He then quizzed me about day-to-day living and the problems I faced. He suggested prescribing a different medication for Norman. This was intended to help people with moderate to severe Alzheimer's disease and worked by slowing down the deterioration and helping to modify behaviour. It is called Ebixa (Mementine) and Norman has continued this medication to his day without any unpleasant side effects. I always found him more aggressive on Aricept and Exelon so the new medication seemed an improvement. There is no real way of knowing if those drugs are doing any good as you do not know how they would have been without them but Norman did seem less excitable on Ebixa.

For a little over a year I had been suffering from a very painful right shoulder. Many years ago I had been knocked down by a car on a zebra crossing and had suffered permanent damage to my left shoulder with very restricted movement of that arm. This probably made me over compensate with my right arm which began to complain. I had tried the usual treatments such as pain control, physiotherapy and Osteopathy with no improvement. I then tried steroid injections, which made it worse if anything and was finally referred to an Orthopaedic Consultant. He did scans and x-rays and thought that he may be able to shave away a bit of bone to help the pain. However when I was having surgery it was noted that there was damage to the rotator cuff and this had to be repaired. This meant that recovery after the operation would take longer as I needed to keep my arm in a sling for 6 weeks. Because of the limitations of my left arm I felt pretty helpless and my daughter in Scotland arranged to come down to help me for a few days. It is interesting that Norman, who had always been sympathetic and supportive on the rare occasions when I was ill, was very indifferent to my predicament. He wanted me to take the sling off and insisted there was nothing wrong with me. I think he must have felt the attention was being taken away from him! To everyone's amusement he behaved extremely well during Nicola's visit and you would hardly have known he was suffering from dementia. I think Nicola thought I was exaggerating his behavioural problems.

Towards the end of Nicola's visit I had taken Norman out for a walk and he decided to return by the short route. It was a beautiful January day and I continued my full three miles. When I got home Norman was not there. I assumed he had gone to Julian's house, which he often did. I set off to find him and noticed that the phone was flashing. This was a message to say that Norman had fallen on his return home and sustained head and facial injuries. An ambulance had been called and he had been taken to Airedale Hospital.

Luckily Julian was around and took Nicola and me straight to Accident and Emergency (A & E). What a mess Norman's poor face was in, he had broken his nose and a couple of teeth. He had deep gashes on his forehead and cheeks and the area around his eyes was swollen. After he was cleaned up and x-rayed his blood pressure was taken and it was decided to keep him in hospital overnight. Whilst this was being arranged we tried to reassure Norman and keep him calm. He decided he needed the toilet and Nicola, who is a Registered General Nurse (RGN), found him a urine bottle. He absolutely refused to use it and started to get off the bed. It took all three of us with all our combined strength to prevent him standing up. He became very angry and abusive and Nicola was finally able to see how difficult he could be to care for when he did not want to co-operate. He was eventually transferred to an assessment ward where a nurse told us he would be monitored and probably transferred to another ward so that he could have tests to find out why he kept fainting. We left him in a very confused and unhappy state.

To our surprise we were contacted by phone at 8.30am the next morning to bring him home. Nicola was due to go home the next day and knew that I could not look after her Dad with two disabled shoulders. The Sister said there was nothing she could do about this and that Norman's medical problems should be sorted out by his G.P. Nicola had a long, heated conversation with the Sister and we were invited to go to the ward for further discussion. Norman was very distressed and excitable when we arrived and had clearly given them a difficult night. He was obviously unwell and in some discomfort with his injuries. After much discussion the Sister finally agreed to keep him one more night and asked if I would like the hospital Social Worker to contact me. I accepted this offer with some trepidation as my experience so far with Social Services had been rather negative. Nicola left for home early next morning after helping me to dress, and I waited quite anxiously for the Social Worker to ring.

What a pleasant surprise when she did. She discussed my needs and Norman's needs. Perhaps it helped that she sympathised about my shoulder as she suffered from severe shoulder pains herself. Anyway she was able to offer some respite care for Norman whilst I was incapacitated, and I arranged to meet her at the hospital in the afternoon. My brother took me along to meet her as, of course, I was unable to drive. The Social Worker had managed to get a place in a local Nursing Home for up to six weeks so that Norman could be looked after properly until I was able to do so. This Home was only a couple of miles from home so I was able to walk there and back to visit him each day. In the event he only stayed for 3 weeks as I missed him terribly and felt I could cope as his injuries healed. I had become quite resourceful during this period and had learned to dress by all sorts of tricks. I could get a sweater over my head by hanging it on a doorknob and sitting on the floor and then slowly raising my head through the neck hole. I had learned to fasten my bra from the front and had become quite adept at coping with the various fastenings of the sling. It was quite cold out being January so I bought a cheap cape for outdoors as it covered the sling quite nicely. I became a real expert at darting up-and-down step ladders at this time as I was unable to reach the overhead kitchen cupboards. I had to rearrange cupboards so that daily essentials were within reach. I did have to compromise on housework a bit but I found it is absolutely amazing what you can do when you have to.

What I could not do was take Norman's weight. Even though he is quite slim I could not help him to take a bath in the usual way and we had to compromise with showers, which he hates, and all over washes. It was difficult to go out for a walk together as Norman refuses to use his walking stick and leans heavily on me. To try to get to the bottom of Norman's fainting spells he was referred to a cardiac consultant who fitted a heart monitor as Norman would not co-operate with an Electrocardiogram (E.C.G.).

This is when I realised that Norman's attitude toward me had changed. He did not like me wearing a sling and wanted me to take it off. He could not understand that I was less capable than usual and became extremely demanding and critical and attention seeking. He was obviously upset that he had had to stay in a Nursing Home and could not understand why he had had to go there. He remembered nothing about his fall and felt his life had been disrupted for no reason at all. This aspect of Alzheimer's disease is very upsetting for the carer as the cared for person becomes very self-engrossed and has no empathy with anyone else's feelings. I spent a lot of time discussing this with him and although he seemed to understand at the time he quickly forgot the discussion and reverted to his demanding behaviour.

I suppose this is when it hit me that we were no longer equal partners in a marriage. I had long accepted that Norman was unable to contribute to the everyday affairs of running a home. He could not deal with the mail or the telephone. He could no longer recognise coins or notes or go to the shop alone. He could not run errands or be relied on to complete a simple task. Luckily I had Power of Attorney for him and was able to deal with all our financial affairs. Being the kind of person I am this did not bother me too much. It bothered me that Norman was failing, but I did not mind the extra tasks. What upset me most was the emotional loss. I could no longer share my feelings with my husband. We were not able to share memories – happy or sad. I couldn't sit down and talk it through if I had had a bad day, or share the joy on happier occasions. He no longer recognised or acknowledged our friends and tried to avoid company in order to save him embarrassment. He had some awareness that he had problems with his memory, but laughed it off as trivial. He seemed to stop showing emotion very much; as though he didn't really feel anything much and nothing affected him. Occasionally he would tell me he loves me and I'm sure he does but he is not able to express this love in shared daily living. So I began to accept my role as his carer rather than his wife, his protector, rather than mutual support and sometimes his slave rather than his companion.

I needed to think about how I was coping with all this, I tried to do a practical evaluation of the skills and qualities needed to look after someone with Alzheimer's and the skills and qualities I possess and then consider what I could do about the shortfall.

I had been expecting a visit from members of the Mental Health Team attached to the consultant Psychiatrist for the elderly. This appointment had already been cancelled once but I was looking forward to advice and support from an occupational therapist, social worker and or nurse. In the end just the social worker arrived. He suggested various activities that might stimulate Norman such as sorting balls of wool into various colours; He thought Norman might be happy with a room of his own where he could follow art and craft activities. Why did I find my hackles rising at these suggestions? I must admit I found it somewhat patronising that a young man with loads of theoretical knowledge about Alzheimer's had very little understanding of the reality of living with it. There was no way that Norman would spend time in a room if I wasn't there and his concentration span was so short that he lost patience with any attempt to get him to start, let along complete, a simple task. He was very happy to watch me doing chores around the home but spent many hours just gazing into space and day dreaming, with which he seemed content. The rest of the time he paced up and down the sitting room or stood looking out of the window.

I certainly did not spend a great deal of time trying to entertain him. Most of it was spent on cooking and cleaning, laundry, shopping, taking him for walks and constantly searching for the many objects he enjoyed hiding. Trying to keep him clean and smart was quite a challenge by now as he began to be incontinent.

All in all I did not find this visit helpful and I have to ask myself whether I am resistant to outside advice. I certainly resist anything that will make my workload greater than it already is or anything that will upset my well worked out routine. This is the OCD bit I suppose, but mainly it is because what I know how to do, I do extremely well. Anything I find too difficult I try to avoid altogether and I certainly hate change. So the practical aspects of looking after Norman I was able to adjust to over time. Behavioural changes and increased demands on my time and patience upset me much more. So I tended to stick to my tried and tested ways of coping and largely ignored "outside" advice.

Having said that, I did realise that Norman must be bored. By now he was unable to follow television programmes and frequently asked me to switch it off. He was probably frustrated because everything moved too fast for his brain to follow. In retrospect I wonder if he might have enjoyed children's programmes better. Although we still took the local evening paper, the Telegraph and Argus, Norman could no longer concentrate to read it. He understood the words but could not understand the meaning of news items. During coffee breaks I would tell him items of news and current affairs that I thought might interest him. He always paid attention and usually made appropriate comments but quickly forgot what we had discussed.

Because I have always enjoyed walking, I did encourage Norman to take exercise in this way. Although not a lover of walking, he preferred to accompany me rather than be left alone. Although this worked well for short walks I have to confess I was much happier walking alone. Not only could I walk faster and further it was lovely to have the opportunity to have some time to myself and think my own thoughts. I have always enjoyed my own company and solved many a problem while out in the fresh air. My other main form of exercise is swimming, and although Norman dislikes the water he was happy to be a spectator a couple of times a week.

We did look at the idea of having a "sitter" to stay at home with Norman whilst I ventured out and were visited at home to discuss this. Norman was not at all keen on the idea of being with a stranger He tends to be a private person anyway but I think he realised that he was having difficulty keeping up a conversation and felt embarrassed. For my part I did not like the idea of someone else making cups of tea in my kitchen. The thoughts of anyone making free with my home and equipment feels like an invasion on my privacy and this is also probably why I resisted home care later on.

During school holidays it was possible to leave Norman for short periods with Rachel who worked school hours. I could also leave him for short spells with my brother David. I did not do this too often as he can be quite challenging at times. He tended to constantly ask where I was and when I would be returning.

Another "helpful strategy" that neither of us felt we would be comfortable with was attending "group" sessions. Both the Alzheimer's Association and Carers' Resource offered the opportunity to meet other people who shared some of our problems. Norman was absolutely adamant about this and refused to even talk about it. From my point of view I felt that, on the rare occasion's I went out socially, I would prefer to avoid anything to do with illness or Alzheimer's disease. I know that many people gain a lot of support from sharing their experiences with others but it is simply not for me. I have tried to analyse why this is so and can only think that it is partly because I feel I have nothing to offer and partly a sort of arrogance that I can manage on my own.

Like many carers, I realised that I was simply not trained to do this job and looked for organisations that offered this. Training is a lot different from going over the same ground in groups and I wanted a way forward.

Brick walls abound when you become a carer and this was just another example. Carers' Resource had delivered training called "Caring with Confidence" for eighteen months under the governments "New Deal for Carers" strategy. After a change in government the funding was axed and the programme had to be withdrawn. I still feel that it is not beyond the ability of local organisations to set up some kind of pilot scheme to identify the skills and qualities needed in the caring role and to find ways to consolidate strengths and overcome or at least recognise weaknesses. There must be dozens of ways to increase the confidence of people in the caring role. Every carer I have ever spoken to wishes they were a better carer. Well let's get empowered so that we can be!

Because I am not a group person I had to look elsewhere for support as I realised that my mental health was suffering through Norman's illness. However strong you think you are, the day to day experience of coping with a person whose behaviour is unpredictable gives you a hell of a battering. Add to that disturbed nights and a broken sleep pattern and something's got to give.

I spent quite a bit of time moaning to my family about the difficulties I was facing. Whilst they were unable to offer much in the way of practical help I appreciate that they were incredibly supportive. I also realised it was a bit selfish to keep doing this as they all go out to work, and did not need the extra worry of my belly aching. The answer seemed to be to get some counselling. As I had been a counsellor with what is now called Relate in the 1970s I knew the value of engaging in face to face exploration of the complexity of feeling engendered by living in a stressful situation. I knew that there were no quick fix solutions, I knew it might be painful but I liked the confidentiality of it and I had to do something.

Several opportunities for counselling presented themselves but I preferred not to have to pay for this service if possible. My reasons for this are mixed. When I was a counsellor we were all volunteers and the idea of charging clients was just surfacing. I resented this because I didn't feel I wanted anyone to put a monetary value on the service I freely gave, donations okay, but a fee I was not comfortable with. As well as that, an on-going process like counselling can add up to a tidy amount and it is tempting to restrict the number of sessions if you feel it is costing too much. I also felt that I deserved a free service – payback time maybe. It was to be some little while before I got it.

Norman gradually became used to going to day-care. He called it "the hospital" and insisted he stayed in a bed all day. He told me all sorts of weird and wonderful tales when he came home but I think he quite enjoyed the change. I checked to see how he had settled and was told he was very quiet and preferred to watch rather than join in activities. He was picked up at 9am each Wednesday and returned home at 4pm which was quite a break for me. This lasted for six months and then the co-ordinator left and we began to have problems. Sometimes I would have Norman in his outdoor clothing ready to go at 9am and his transport did not turn up until 10am or 10.30am. He was being brought back at 3pm or even earlier, so if I went out, I had to make sure I was back for 2.30pm. Then one day his transport did not turn up at all. I had to weigh up whether I really thought day care was worth it. It doesn't come free, though the amount you pay depends on the income and savings of the client. I decided to cancel further sessions, as by now, I was finding it more difficult to care for Norman at night time than during the day. Norman's routine was to start being restless at about 4am I could usually settle him down after a visit to the toilet but he would be fully awake by 5am. At this point I would get up and go in the bath, asking Norman to stay where he was till I was dressed. More often than not he tried to dress himself, sometimes with comical results. He was very uncooperative about having a bath or wash at this time but did insist on a thorough shave with his electric razor. This gave me chance to start breakfast and we were usually eating before six.

When he had eaten it was easier to persuade him to attend to hygiene matters but he was inclined to be less than thorough. I have never known anyone make a tube of toothpaste last as long as Norman can! After, he would sit and watch TV while I got on with the chores of the day. Later in the morning we would go for a walk, or if he wasn't bothered I would go on my own. We would then have a cup of coffee together before I started lunch. In the afternoons we might get on a bus to town or further afield. As I started to get broken nights it was quite useful to let him have the window seat so that I could safely nod off next to him. After our tea or evening meal he would start to get restless and start walking up and down the sitting room. No matter how often I asked him to sit down he was quite excitable at this time. Sometimes he strayed outside when I was not paying attention and wandered off. By 8pm he was quite tired and asking to go to bed. I tried to keep him up till about 9pm, then he had a drink and his tablets and I settled him for sleep. I would usually read downstairs for an hour or so. At one time that was it until 4am but more recently he began to get up in the night and trail all over the house. Sometimes he was looking for the toilet. Sometimes he was looking for "the lads", or a cat or dog. I learned to wake up when I felt him moving but he was very stubborn and would not cooperate with me. On a couple of occasions he was on his way out of the back door so I had to hide the keys after that.

It was probably around this time that what little patience I have grew very thin and I began to shout at him. At first it was quite effective. If I said "sit down" in a loud voice he did as I asked. The trouble was 10 seconds later he was up again. It was much like caring for a very naughty child but who was much bigger than I was. He was unable to learn from being "told off" and kept repeating the same annoying behaviour such as emptying his wardrobe or filling the bath to overflowing with cold water and putting the towels in. Of course I felt guilty at shouting at him for an illness he had no control over but I came to realise that it didn't to seem to bother him and at least it was an outlet for my frustration. I had been seeing my gynaecologist about a residual problem from the prolapse repair I had had two years ago. This was a very irritable bladder. It was proposed to try to enlarge the bladder under anaesthetic and to remove some adhesions. This was a day-care operation but I needed time to recover and I now had contact with a lovely social worker who was able to arrange for three night's respite care for Norman. Arranging respite care at short notice is not easy as care homes cannot always accommodate short stay residents. We went to look at the home and it seemed very bright and modern with a huge conservatory. Norman seemed to like the look of it but did not understand why he had to stay there.

So, Julian and I dropped him off on the day of my surgery and then I was deposited at the hospital, Sister would let Julian know when I was ready to be taken home.

I was not ready to leave the hospital till about 7pm and Julian had just finished his meal when the call came. He and Rachel set off at 7pm and I was rather concerned when it got to 7.30pm and they had not arrived as we only live 10 minutes away from the hospital. It was

69

about 7.45pm when the nurse informed me that my son had arrived. To my surprise it was Andrew, not Julian who came to pick me up. He explained that Julian and Rachel had been diverted by a phone call from the Home to say that Norman had absconded and the Police had been informed. Because of the anaesthetic I was unable to help in the search for him and was quite frantic with worry as he had been missing for several hours. Apparently, a visitor had let him out. I had explained to the Home staff that he was inclined to wander and would get out if he could but they assured me they had a good security system.

By now several friends and relatives were involved in the search. It was Julian who eventually found him about three miles from the Home. He had walked to Farnhill where he lived in his youth. Whether he intended to go there or it was a coincidence we will never know as he seemed very confused when he was found and could not tell the police where he had been. Coming on top of the operation I was quite upset by this incident and Julian kindly stayed the night to look after me.

When I went to collect Norman a couple of days later I noticed that he looked very unkempt and was wearing the same shirt as the day I took him in. He was smelly and I brought him home and bathed him and threw all his clothes in the washing machine. When his social worker phoned to ask how Norman had gone on in the Home I voiced my concerns. She must have made a report about the incident, because I eventually received a letter from the Home to the effect that Norman had been doubly incontinent whilst he was there and that he had urinated in other resident's bedrooms. They insisted that his clothes had been changed and that it was the fault of a visitor that he left the premises.

This incident made me very nervous of respite care. I knew I was reaching the stage when I was going to have to ask for respite breaks but I just kept putting it off.

When you live with an Alzheimer's sufferer day after day and night after night you are not in the best position to realise the effect this is having on your health. It's true that at times I thought I was going mad, but it took the family to realise when I had had enough and that for Norman's sake as well as mine some action had to be taken.

When Norman's social worker got in touch with me to see how I was after the surgery we talked about regular sessions of respite care. The problem was finding a place that was secure enough to ensure that Norman didn't "escape". We looked at a lovely local authority home but the person in charge felt it was not entirely suitable for Norman as it was very close to a main road, a railway line and a canal. The social worker suggested a place which deals entirely with people with Dementia of one kind or another. I have to admit I went to look at this place with a lot of prejudice. Any institution which cares for people who have mental problems attracts a certain kind of reputation in the neighbourhood and I had heard tales of screaming and extreme behaviour. However, Norman seemed to feel comfortable there and there was an easy going sort of atmosphere. True, the place could do with updating and a bit of money spending on it but in the present recession it is not going to happen. Julian and Rachel liked the feel of the place and we agreed that

Norman would spend one week in six there if the social worker could get the funding. Norman was not in a financial position to pay all his own fees so we had to be means tested as with the day care.

So he went in there with some trepidation on my part, but seemed to settle very quickly. In contrast to his timetable at home, he went to bed extremely late, got up late and wandered interminably around the building looking for a way out. The building is quite spacious with a courtyard garden so there was lots of space for him to wander. There was an extremely efficient security system. From my point of view, I felt relaxed about Norman but did not know quite what to do with myself at home. I got lots of jobs done and tried to get used to the idea of being alone in the house at night time. As I am rather deaf I had never noticed all the noises that go on in a house, but once on my own I noticed every little creak. We had previously arranged with Julian and Rachel that the four of us would have a break in Paris for a few days in August. We had already paid for the hotels and ferry crossing and Julian was going to drive down to make it easier for his Dad, rather than flying or the train. We had made this trip for the past 3 years as we are all rather addicted to impressionist paintings not to mention French food and wine. By now it had become patently obvious that Norman was totally unfit to travel and I suggested that Julian and Rachel went alone, but they were concerned that I was utterly exhausted and needed the break. We tried to look at ways to make it possible for me to go with them.

In my innocence, I expected Norman to be really happy to be home after a week in respite but he was quite confused and upset and his incontinence had worsened. He seemed quite bewildered by the geography at home and was unable to find a toilet on his own. I tried to keep to a compromise bed time routine, hoping I could get him to sleep between 10pm and 6am but he was very erratic. He now wanted to get up several times in the night and wandered around downstairs looking for Heaven knows what. He did not always recognise me in the middle of the night and could be quite stubborn and resistant to attempts to get him back to bed.

It was Nicola, our daughter in Scotland who contacted the social worker to express concerns about my health. Nicola had not actually seen her Dad or me since January but the boys had passed on their worries to her. Nicola is a Nurse and has a no-nonsense approach to problems and she felt that I needed intervention from the family as I could not go on like this.

The social worker arranged to call and see us and Julian said he wanted to be present. He didn't mess about. I'll never forget his words "My mum is not capable of looking after my Dad". I was shocked as I had been looking after him for the last four years. He went on to say that I had obsessive compulsive traits and this was making it more difficult for both of us. He felt that I would not be able to take care of Norman at home much longer. The social worker thought that a package of respite breaks might solve the problem, but Julian was adamant that this was no longer enough. He felt that I had asked for too little too late. There was quite a long dialogue about Norman's needs and mine. I had probably not been entirely honest with our social worker as I tried to give the impression I could manage.

Quite apart from all this, the thought of Norman going into permanent care was quite shocking. Yes I had realised that someday it would happen but not yet. It took some while for the implications to hit me. The Social Worker went away to consider the best way forward. If Social Services were to contribute to Norman's care there had to be a formal assessment of his needs. It was agreed that Norman would go back to his respite Home for four weeks in order for this assessment to be done. This allowed me to go to Paris if I wanted to. I was very unsure, but in the end I went. I can honestly say I had a wonderful time. Of course I missed Norman but I was kept so busy I didn't have time to think about him too much. It was just the nights that were a bit of a trial but I'm sure the break did me good. I was feeling better anyway because I was now able to get an unbroken night's sleep.

In the middle of July, the Queen came to Saltaire, which is a World Heritage Site. This was part of the Diamond Jubilee Celebrations and, as Norman has always admired the Royal family, I asked if he would like to go and watch her drive past. Saltaire is only about eight miles from home and was easy to reach by bus. It was a beautiful day and we set off in good time to get a cup of coffee and find ourselves an excellent spot from which to get a good view of the Queen driving past and then getting out of the car to enter the mill she had come to visit. We had to stand a short while but there was a lovely atmosphere and Norman seemed quite content. I kept reminding him who we had come to see and on each occasion he looked quite surprised. Suddenly there was an excited murmur from the crowd and the Royal car drove quite close to us with the Queen and the Duke waving. I turned to make sure Norman was watching, just in time to see him collapse slowly to the ground. Luckily, there was a Police Woman nearby and she was able to summon help. Because of the occasion I had to answer quite a few security questions whilst at the same time trying to activate the hand unit of Norman's heart monitor. Eventually a paramedic arrived who took Norman's blood pressure and did an E.C.G. and immediately sent for an ambulance. By now we were getting nearly as much attention as the Queen! When Norman's blood pressure went up a bit we were taken to Airedale Hospital where they were aware of his history.

The A & E doctor felt that Norman should be kept overnight as the difference between his sitting and standing blood pressure was too great. His heart monitor was checked and although it showed some alteration in rhythm it was not enough to concern the cardiac people.

After my previous experience of Norman staying in Airedale overnight I expected an early morning phone call to bring him home. I eventually phoned them at 11am to be told to phone back after 2pm and then I could probably fetch him home. When I went to the hospital I was diverted to a ward sister who explained that Norman had been very confused and upset during the night. Because he was diagnosed as having postural hypotension the consultant had decided to discontinue one of his prostate medications as this had a side effect of causing postural hypotension. She explained that Norman might now experience urinary retention and have to have a permanent catheter. I knew he would not cope well with this. He had already pulled off 24 hour blood pressure machines and E.C.G. apparatus. As he was due to go into the care home for his four weeks assessment I was very concerned.

The staff at the home however, seemed quite relaxed about it and said they would take it step by step. In the event, he did not have urinary retention, rather the reverse, passing copious amounts of urine that he could no longer control. This was when I contacted the district nurse to arrange for him to have a full supply of incontinence products.

Poor Norman, as if he didn't have enough problems with the Alzheimer's without having fainting attacks and incontinence to deal with. Actually he wasn't really aware of any of this and if there was discomfort when he hurt himself when he fainted, he quickly forgot it. Unfortunately I didn't. I was really quite severely stressed by now and I admit quite looking forward to four weeks respite to get myself sorted out.

After I returned from Paris I sorted out a few chores I had got behind with. I didn't know what to do about the mattress on our bed which had been accidentally soaked on a couple of occasions. Even after removing the stain with a concoction of biological stain remover and bleach I was not happy about what had got inside the mattress and did not feel comfortable sleeping on it. Eventually I invested in a new mattress.

It is not very pleasant sleeping next to someone who is incontinent. I could have moved into the spare room but then I would not have heard Norman getting out of bed during the night. I had to dash round to his side of the bed to stop him getting out too quickly and causing a fainting attack. If I was lucky I could settle him down again, but increasingly he was confused and restless and would not get back into bed.

The four weeks did me good in many ways. I was able to sleep right through the night. For the first few nights I seemed to sleep night and day as though to catch up for all the broken nights. I still found myself waking at 4.30am through, unable to get back to sleep. I was able to go for really long walks, sometimes alone, sometimes with my brother. When I was with David I could talk freely about all my concerns and he was content to listen. I think he felt it was nice that he could support me for a change. I was much calmer and able to think things through in a more rational way. I found time to get my hair done and catch up with personal shopping. It was nice to visit friends on my own without having to think about getting Norman home. It was at this point that the assessment home where Norman was staying was able to offer me counselling. This is a free service offered by relate and funded by the local council to support carers. I really appreciated this. As I began to feel better I tried to look at ways I could cope better when Norman came home. I was quite optimistic.

Towards the end of the assessment a meeting was arranged with the Home assessor, the social worker, Julian and me. I was very nervous about it, partly as I was not sure what I wanted the outcome to be. However, it quickly became apparent that Norman needed 24 hour care and this was not something I could provide on my own at home. The social worker said that my needs had to be considered as well as Norman's and that she would recommend to the social care panel that some funding would be allocated for Norman to go into permanent care. She suggested in the meantime that we look round some local care homes to try to find one that would suit Norman. I think both Julian and I would have liked him to stay at Holmewood where he had settled so well during the assessment period. There was plenty of room for him to roam, an excellent security system and the staff were warm and friendly. Unfortunately, Holmewood is gradually changing into being a short stay centre instead of a permanent Home. They agreed to keep him there until we found a suitable place as it would have confused Norman even more to have come home and then had to move again.

Our first priority when looking for a place for Norman was security. After the experience at the Silsden Home where a visitor innocently let Norman out we were very careful about this. One Home said on the phone that they had an excellent security system, yet when I went to visit I walked straight in as the door had been propped open! Another was a lovely place that Norman would have loved, but right next to a main road. Rachel and I did most of the searching with Julian joining us in the evenings. In the end we settled for a rather large Home which has several wings and a very efficient security system. It was within walking distance of home and, importantly, they had a place available in a shared room. I was not happy about the shared room but was told that if a single room became available he could have it at an extra cost of £25 per week.

We now had to await the decision of the funding panel before we could confirm acceptance of the placement. I was relieved that this was straight forward and, subject to another financial assessment we could make arrangements with the new Home for Norman's admission. An appointment was made for the financial assessor to visit me at home. It was a 4pm appointment which was useful as Julian was able to be present. This was not a happy experience. I had sat down and worked out exactly how much Norman would have to pay toward his fees. This basically is the total amount of his state pension plus one half of his occupational and private pensions. He would also forfeit his attendance allowance which had been paid at the higher rate. Had Norman been able to fund his own care, without a contribution from Social Services he would still haven been entitled to attendance allowance. I went for a walk to clear my head before the appointment and when I returned there was a message on my answerphone from the financial assessor saying she had had a cancellation and would like to do her visit earlier. I phoned her on her mobile to say I had just got in at 3.30pm so we kept to the original 4pm arrangement and she did her shopping!

Her manner was, to say the least rather officious and overbearing. The first thing she needed to know was how much Norman had in savings. This only counted savings in his name and a half of anything in our joint names. If this came to more than £23,500 he would have to pay his own fees with no contribution from social services. If this figure came to between £14,500 and £23,500 he would have to contribute a portion of the difference. She then looked at Norman's income, scribbled some figures on a piece of paper and asked me what the Home charged. I told her it was the same amount as social services allowed but she said that could not be right and we would have to pay a top up fee. She said the social worker had not given me the correct information and I should contact the Home. She also stated that Norman would have to pay a levy as he had too much savings, but that was because she had included the whole of the joint account in her calculations instead of just Norman's half. When she finally produced figures showing how much Norman would have to contribute to his care it was exactly the same figure as I had worked out for myself. Both Julian and I were quite exhausted when she left. An experience like this does help you to appreciate how very sensitive and supportive most people we have come across have been.

Having sorted out Norman's finances I now had to sort out my own. When we were young and poor with four children I opted to pay the reduced married women's National Insurance contribution. This meant that when I reached pension age I was paid a reduced pension based on my husband's contributions. I do have a small occupational pension, plus a half of Norman's tiny occupational pension, but all of this amounts to way less than half of what we had as a couple. So either I got a job or I began to eat into our meagre savings, I daren't even think about Christmas when we have 9 Grandchildren! But the most important thing was to get Norman into a settled environment where he could have his care needs provided 24 hours a day.

I took my husband into a care home on 24th August 2012. I have tried to give an accurate account of the circumstances that led to this momentous decision and I hope my experiences may be of assistance to anyone interested in the progression of Alzheimer's disease, I hope it will bring comfort to carers, who, like me are less than perfect, but struggling with the reality of someone losing not just their memory but their whole personality.

Chapter 6:

Life after Caring

So I came home and sat down and cried my eyes out. I tried to do practical tasks such as sorting out suitable clothing to take to the Home but I simply could not bear to open Norman's wardrobe. I suppose there are some similarities to the feelings you have after bereavement as it is a bereavement of a kind. The shell of the person is still there, they look the same, but the essential qualities that made them the person you love, who you lived your whole life around have slowly withered away. I think I was still in a state of denial to some extent. When I first thought that residential care was a possibility it was as a distant event at some indefinable time in the future. I never attempted to go and look around care homes or send for their literature and I certainly never discussed the idea of care homes with Norman. I suppose deep in my heart I knew that Norman was too badly advanced in his illness for me to be able to care for him at home. But I felt a complete failure and that I should have tried harder and continued to care for him for longer. Now that I was no longer providing all the little services that add up to 24 hour care I was absolutely lost. This gave me more time to think of all my failings. All the irritating behaviour caused by his illness suddenly seemed not so important. I just wanted to go to the Home and fetch him back.

I also had to get used to the idea of being on my own in the night time when I sometimes have vivid dreams and can be quite scared. Whereas his physical presence by my side had been so reassuring I now had to cope alone. It didn't help that I have hearing problems and was confused by unfamiliar noises that I had not noticed before. I was still in the "wake-up early" mode which I had adopted to fit in with Norman's wakefulness and kept myself as busy as possible catching up on neglected chores. I had never done much decorating, leaving this to Norman, but decided the pantry looked dingy and gave it a coat of paint. I was so impressed with the result that I gradually went through the whole house on a revival mission. When I look back, Norman had not been able to do tasks of this kind for a very long time but we had been so caught up in his illness we didn't notice the shabbiness. My brother had helped me to transform our bedroom into a brighter fresher place to wake up to. Unfortunately Norman was only able to sleep there for about a month before he transferred to care.

I can't remember who advised me not to visit Norman in the Home every day. I was told that it would make it more difficult for Norman to settle and more difficult for me. I'm not sure I agree with this from Norman's point of view as he has no concept of time and tends to think that I live there with him. He often told me that the lady in the next chair was his wife! He seemed to recognise me but often thought I was his mother. It is true that it was difficult to hold a conversation with him, so mostly I just told him what I had been doing and bits and bobs about the family. He told me about his day but it was largely nonsense. A lot of the events he described were hallucinatory and frequently to do with animals. He said he had a dog and it was lost. I asked the dog's name and he got irritable and said he only called it "dog". I tried to set a pattern of visiting on alternate days and encouraged other family members to visit on different days.

One of the things that disturbed me was the sad state of some of the residents who were more advanced in the illness than Norman was and often had physical difficulties too. Although communication was difficult I tried to get to know their names and to acknowledge them on my visits. One particular lady took it upon herself to "look after" Norman and walk up and down the corridor with him. He seemed to accept this quite happily. Seeing people in very advanced stages of Dementia was quite depressing as it made me very aware of the progress of the disease and I could only relate it to how Norman might deteriorate.

Visiting hours at the home are quite free and I tried to call at different hours of the day. I usually found Norman more alert in the earlier part of the day and more confused toward the evening. The staff told me that he becomes more restless in the evenings and wanders up and down the long corridor. He does not seem to welcome visitors at that time.

I couldn't fail to notice some deterioration in Norman's condition after he moved into care. He became doubly incontinent which seemed very sudden as we had only had urinary incontinence at home and then usually in the night. He was also less mobile and seemed to have difficulty getting out of his chair. He developed a skin rash due to the incontinence and also got a chest infection. He suffered from very painful gout from time to time. The doctor was called on each occasion and prescriptions given. The staff all seem very conscientious and friendly and seem quite fond of Norman which makes me feel better.

I thought it would be a treat for both of us if I could take him into town to get his hair cut and then have a coffee together. I really looked forward to this as a means of being together as a couple for a while, how we used to be. Alas it did not turn out that way. I had great difficulty in getting him down the stairs of the Home and into the car. He fought with the seat belt and it took quite a while to get him settled. He was quite good in the barbers' shop but got excited when we were outside. He could not recognise the town where he had lived the largest part of his life but said he would enjoy a cup of coffee. I got him into the Coop where there is lots of space in the restaurant and sat him down at a table hoping he would not disappear while I got the drinks! All was well until he decided to butter his own scone. Instead he buttered the plate and the table, threw the scone on the floor and ate the jam! Luckily, there were not many people in the café. He then needed the toilet and before I could get him organised, had weed on the floor! By now I think we had both had enough so we shuffled back to the car and I felt nothing but relief when I got him safely back to the Home. As I was leaving him there he said "I thought you said we were going out"! Not a happy experience but it did me one favour; I suddenly realised that I had no need to feel guilty. He was a very confused man with severe Alzheimer's disease who could behave quite unpredictably at times. I am a very slight 74 year old woman, five foot in stilettoes and simply did not have the stamina to cope any more. I had obviously expected far too much of both of us on this occasion and it would not be wise to plan further excursions without another pair of hands.

I was so concerned about Norman settling in his new environment that I didn't think much about how I would settle with the Home. When your loved one goes into permanent care you are going to see an awful lot of that Home and you need to feel alright about it. I did feel that we had not had an awful lot of time to look at different Homes as it was felt wiser to have a straight transfer from his assessment placement to his permanent Home rather than coming home in between which would have confused him. Because our main concern was security so that Norman could not endanger himself by leaving the premises we were very limited. The local authority seem to be closing down or re-adapting its residential E.M.I. (elderly mentally infirm) units so we were forced to look at the private Homes. The next main concern was the cost. We needed a Home that would accept the local authority rate for Norman's level of care. Lesser concerns were the proximity to where I live so that I could visit regularly and whether Norman could have a room to himself. Norman needs plenty of space to wander up and down so that was another factor. I had to be realistic and accept that nowhere was going to be perfect. Most of his needs were met by the Home we chose except that he could not have a single room unless we were prepared to pay another £25 per week. Social Services were unable to fund this and the Home would not negotiate so at present he has to share until I find a way to solve this problem. Sharing a room when you are doubly incontinent is not a very pleasant prospect for either occupant. To be fair, Norman does not complain but in his life before Alzheimer's he would have categorically refused to share a room with a stranger.

I suppose you never think that your loved one is being cared for quite like he was at home. No one person can give him one-to-one attention throughout the day and night and whilst the carers seem quite fond of Norman he doesn't get the emotional support or the warmth and cuddles that we shared together. It's not easy for us to have a cuddle at the Home as there is no privacy. It's true that I was very exasperated with Norman's illness and shouted at him in frustration but he always got instant attention to his needs.

So, I think I am still adjusting to the ways of a Care Home. To make things a little easier I attend a monthly social group at the Home to try to get to know more about how the Home runs and meet other carers.

There was a final review between the unit manager, the social worker, Norman and myself after he had been there a month. I requested that Norman have an extra bath each week and asked why the toilet was kept locked as I felt he would use it at least some of the time if it was open.

Because the wing housed people in various stages of Dementia it was likely that the toilet would be misused and it was felt it was better that residents only used the toilet under supervision. So I got the extra bath for Norman but the toilet stays locked which does not help his incontinence. Although it was agreed at this meeting to try to get a single room for Norman, nothing so far has come of this. Norman said he was quite happy and enjoyed his meals. I have no doubt about this as he has an excellent appetite and can be quite greedy if there are second helpings. He has certainly put on some weight whilst in care and this must be partly due to the fact that he gets very little physical exercise.

I think I have come to the conclusion that nowhere would be perfect for Norman. Homes after all are businesses and although the staff are kind it feels rather impersonal.

Another aspect of Home life that disturbed me was the fact that after being in control of every aspect of Norman's life for such a long time I was suddenly dispensable. After preparing his meals, attending to hygiene, doing his laundry, sorting out his medication, dealing with incontinence products and sorting out his finances I was suddenly redundant. I simply handed over a pile of clothing, the nappies, the tablets and my husband and that was that! Now all I have to do for him is worry about him, visit, cut his nails and take him for haircuts – and still sort out his finances. It just feels all too sudden as it is hard to put down tasks you have done for a long time.

Quite apart from adjusting to Norman being in a Home I had and still have to cope with living like a single person after all these years together. Widows have to adjust to this situation all the time and my friends who are widowed find it difficult to understand how I could ever have let Norman go into a Home. Of course they do. They have suffered major loss and would have yearned for a short while longer together, while I seem to have abandoned Norman. What perhaps is hard for them to grasp is that Norman, the real Norman, who I fell in love with, married, had children with, grew old with, who was my whole world, has been lost to me for quite a long time.

As the dark nights draw in I do sometimes feel rather lonely in the evenings. After tea I usually tidy up, finish any odd jobs, watch the 6 o'clock news and settle down with a good book. I have noticed that I have suddenly developed a sweet tooth and find myself munching chocolate or fudge at this time. It's probably comfort eating but I need to keep it under control. During the day I can keep busy with household chores, shopping, swimming, walking and visiting Norman. Christmas is on its way so there are puddings and cakes to make for the family plus budgeting for all the presents.

Our oldest son Ian has looked into the possibility of "continuing care" for Norman which would mean that the NHS would fund his care. There are strict guidelines for claiming continuing care and Norman does have other health needs apart from his Alzheimer's.

Nevertheless it is important that we try to get everything we can to make life as comfortable and enjoyable as possible for him and it's sad that this mostly comes down to money. So pursuing this matter will keep me busy and on my toes and I have Ian to support me.

Through Carers Resource I have been offered a short break in the countryside and I really look forward to this. A couple of nights away in a converted Railway Station in the Yorkshire Dales sounds wonderful. I am allowed to take a friend so it will be a nice change. As yet I don't feel able to go away for more than a day or two so perhaps this break will give me more confidence to go further afield. This break is provided free through the generosity of the Rotary club.

Perhaps my biggest support, apart from my family has been the on-going counselling that I was able to access through the Relate, Bradford caring and sharing project at the Holmewood Centre. This is presently funded by the local authority to support carers and the counsellors are trained Relate personnel. I have fully appreciated the opportunity to offload all the distress and frustration that has built up especially during the last couple of years. I quite expected a confrontational approach as I was feeling so very guilty when I first saw my counsellor. In fact the whole experience has been quite uplifting.

Gill was able to help me see that I have spent my whole life caring for other people and have sometimes neglected to look after myself. I probably don't really know how and am having to learn. I have certainly never been in a position to pamper myself and I don't think I would enjoy this. What gives me great satisfaction is the pleasure I get from a job well done. So I'm going to have to choose jobs that are pleasurable aren't I? I still see Gill every two or three weeks as she thinks I need support during this difficult transitional period.

As the situation has some parallel with bereavement I also had a couple of sessions with Cruse at the suggestion of Sarah from Carers' Resource. This helped me to confront the issues of loss I have experienced.

I finally succumbed to Andrew's suggestion that I have his old computer. Like many people my age, I have always resisted getting involved in modern technology. Learning how to use it should keep me out of mischief and maybe help me get my story typed up.

Then, just as I was beginning to relax about Norman being in care he had an unfortunate experience. One way or another he managed to leave his unit around 7am. How he got down the stairs I will never know, but he did and then he walked out of the front door. He walked half a mile toward a major road and luckily was noticed by a member of staff coming on duty. He was quickly taken back to his wing. As yet I am unable to establish how he got out or even whether he was dressed. Naturally, the whole family are very upset about this and the Sister on the wing has promised that he will be more closely observed to prevent this happening again. I have persuaded him to wear his identity bracelet which I bought him last Christmas. At least it has my phone number and Julian's mobile number which should quickly alert us if he strays. This was a very unsettling experience, though Norman remembers nothing about it.

When Norman was at home I used to give him a multi vitamin and a 500mg vitamin C tablet every day. Of course this is not practicable in the Home and I wonder if this is partly why he picks up more infections. He seems to have a persistent chest infection which seemed to be aggravated by his anti-flu injection and made him feel quite poorly for a day or two. I can't recall him ever having a chest infection during our married life. I suppose also that infections travel like wild fire where elderly people live together.

The Home where Norman lives is bright and modern. From outside it looks more like a hotel and is fresh and inviting. It is a large place which seems to be run according to the book and there are quite firm rules. The care staff receive in-service training and from what I have seen form good relationships with the residents and are genuinely concerned about them. So, whilst I find it difficult to adjust to Norman being there I accept that the level of care is good and that Norman is perfectly happy.

Chapter 7:

Moving On

So, we have come a long way since Norman couldn't remember asking me to get some "Special K" cereal for his lunch. To anyone caring for someone in the earlier stages of dementia it must sound quite depressing. But there have been many happy occasions during those twelve years. For at least half of that time there was very little noticeable change at all, and when Norman had memory lapses they were often sprinkled with humour, and they didn't interfere in Norman's life in any way. It is only during the last three or four years that his personality has progressively changed and he has gradually lost the ability to complete simple everyday tasks. Generally speaking, he is still very polite and considerate of other people. Most days, when I visit he seems happy to see me, and even though he does not always recognise me as his wife, he knows that he has strong feeling for me and on odd occasions tells me he loves me. Our relationship is actually better since he has been in care because I am not fraught with all the problems his illness brings and we are calm and comfortable together. He is a lovely Man. Alzheimer's disease is an ugly illness. For the sake of my children and everybody else's children I hope the breakthrough will not be long in coming. There may never be a complete cure but we may be able to relieve many of the features of this distressing condition. My heart goes out to all carers who have to watch the slow deterioration of the mental capacity of a loved one. Most of all I grieve for the sufferer who is unable to brighten his or her autumn years with a lifetime of wonderful memories.

Chapter 8:

The Lesson

So what have I learned from all this? Well, certainly writing it all down has shown me what I could have done better. I can see now the things that have helped me and what has hindered. The main mistake I made was in not getting help sooner. I thought I could go it alone but I had no idea what was in store for me and how challenging caring for someone with Alzheimer's disease can be. If I had not let myself get so worn out I would have been in a better position to be assertive when people tried to block my attempts to get support.

It might be easier to make a list of the positive and negative aspects of my experience.

What has helped:-

- Support of family and friends
- My own good health (at least physically)
- Eventually, a helpful Social Worker
- Having a registered Power of Attorney
- Holidays in Goa – something to look forward to

- Sympathetic G.P.
- Skilled and experienced counsellors
- Qualities such as:-
  o Tenacity
  o Optimism
  o Sense of humour
  o Good organising skills
  o Strength of mind

What has hindered:-

- Poor front line social service staff
- Insensitivity from professionals
- Difficulty in getting a diagnosis
- My ignorance about the disease (Dr Tom Smith's book did help)
- My hesitation in accepting Nursing Home Care due to previous experience with my mother and mother-in-law. Also the financial implications
- Personal characteristics such as:-
  o Impatience
  o Intolerance
  o Obsession with tidiness and order
  o Pride
  o Independence carried too far

Chapter 9:

Why Did I Write My Story?

Primarily, writing it all down was a kind of therapy. My thoughts and feelings were all jumbled and I certainly feel better for getting it all on paper. The task has also helped to keep my mind focused during a period when I felt very confused and abandoned.

As I read through the way the progress of the disease affected both of us I realise that are thousands of people going through the same process who will relate to many of my experiences. If it helps someone, just a little, I will be humbly grateful and amply rewarded.

Where I go from here depends on me. At the moment I take one day at a time. People tell me I have got my life back and so I have the freedom to begin to socialise again. I have the opportunity to learn new skills and to help others. I need to open myself up to change and accept new challenges.

I will always treasure the memories of my life with Norman. I am so grateful that I can.

Forget me not.

By Mary Jennings

Acknowledgements

What started as an attempt to come to terms with Norman going into care by writing down my thoughts and feelings became something else when I shared parts of it with other people. From their response came the idea of "Forget me Not" and I would sincerely like to thank the people who made it possible.

They include:

Julie and Jessica, who grappled with my appalling hand writing and managed to turn a dog-eared script into something resembling a manuscript.

Sarah and Stella from The carers' Resource, who encouraged and supported me to persist in getting the book published and corrected my errors. Also Liz who patiently typed out the documents I needed.

Tim, who has already published his work and gave me lots of advice.

Yvonne, for sharing her experience in getting her own books published and for taking the time to read my story and share her comments.

I would especially like to thank my family for patiently reading through the script and adding their thoughts. Last, but not least, thank you to my Grandson, Charlie who designed the lovely cover, which cleverly depicts forget-me not flowers degenerating into D.N.A.

If I have forgotten anyone, please accept my apologies.